Original title:
The Ocean's Warmth

Copyright © 2025 Creative Arts Management OÜ
All rights reserved.

Author: Robert Ashford
ISBN HARDBACK: 978-1-80581-527-3
ISBN PAPERBACK: 978-1-80581-054-4
ISBN EBOOK: 978-1-80581-527-3

Currents of Nostalgia

Waves giggle as they splash around,
Tickling toes upon the ground.
Seagulls squawk like they're on a quest,
Searching for fries, they know the best!

Sandy castles, built with pride,
Melting down with the rising tide.
Flushed-faced kids in a water race,
Belly flops and giggles fill the space.

Floating on rafts, we're kings of the sea,
Until a dolphin steals your iced tea.
Jellyfish dance, with their bizarre flair,
Their squishy antics are quite the scare!

With sunlight glinting on a bubbly brew,
We reminisce about the silly things we'd do.
So we laugh and play, till the day is done,
In this salty embrace, we're forever young!

Tides of Comfort

When splashing about, we lose our hats,
The seagulls laugh, like cheeky brats.
We dive headfirst, but come up slow,
With seaweed wigs, we're quite the show.

The fish all giggle, make bubbles galore,
As we tumble around on the sandy floor.
With each big wave, we try to eat,
Sandwiches mixed with a side of sea treat!

Embrace of Waves

The waves come in like a friendly friend,
They splash us hard, then around they spin.
My flip-flops fly, caught in their dance,
We all end up drenched, but what a chance!

Mermaids giggle at our clumsy fall,
While crabs in tuxedos waltz down the hall.
With each salty splash, we burst into laughter,
Sandy and wet, we crave more disaster!

Sea's Gentle Caress

Oh what joy in the sea's soft seat,
Jumping like dolphins, can't be beat.
But when waves crash, our shorts get a tug,
Sandy and soaked, we give a shrug.

The jellyfish wave, all jelly and bright,
As we splash around till near the twilight.
With each gentle roll, our worries unwind,
Floating like corks, not a care on our mind!

Warmth Beneath the Surface

Submerged we go, beneath the blue,
Encountering fish asking, 'Who are you?'
We wiggle our toes, don't quite belong,
As dolphins join in with a joyous song.

The tide pulls us in for a silly ride,
Making funny faces, can't hide our pride.
On this grand stage, we play our part,
With laughter bubbling up from the heart!

Radiance in the Salt Air

Seagulls squawk as they dance,
Sandcastles rise with a chance.
Suntan lotion on my nose,
I smell like a pickle, I suppose.

Flip-flops slapping on the beach,
Chasing waves that are out of reach.
Kids squeal as they take a dive,
It's pure chaos, yet we thrive.

Shady umbrellas sway with glee,
Ice cream melting, sticky spree.
Sunburned backs and mismatched socks,
Beach days come with silly knocks.

As the tide rolls in and out,
We laugh and shout, without a doubt.
With every wave that seems so grand,
We play a game of catch, oh man!

A Symphony of Surf

Coconut drinks with little straws,
Ocean splashes, applause and jaws.
Crabs scuttle, trying to hide,
We giggle at their sideways stride.

A surfboard's laugh fills the air,
One wipeout leads to quite a scare.
Fins and floaties bob around,
Each splash is a joy, laughter's sound.

Naked toes, the sand's embrace,
Sandy sandwiches, quite the chase.
A dolphin peeks to take a look,
Then swims away like a storybook.

The sun bows down, a golden show,
We dance on waves, let our light glow.
With every beat, we feel so free,
Life's a symphony by the sea.

Cradle of the Coral

Underwater secrets we explore,
Where fish wear hats, we can't ignore.
Turtles glide with a groovy style,
Coral reefs look like a smile.

Amidst the seaweed, treasures hide,
A crab in pajamas takes a ride.
Starfish sparkly, like tiny shows,
Bubbles pop like circus goes.

A jellyfish floats, what a sight!
Looks like he's dancing in the light.
Shells may chatter, gossip so divine,
As seahorses sip on brine.

In this cradle of aqua charm,
We laugh, we splash, we mean no harm.
The whims of water make us cheer,
What a funny world down here!

Lullabies of the Sea

The waves sing softly, a soothing tune,
While crabs tap dance beneath the moon.
Seafoam giggles on the shore,
With whispers of tales from yonder more.

Breezes carry salty jokes,
As dolphins perform their silly strokes.
Starry nights bring dreams anew,
Of sandy castles and sky so blue.

A starfish yawns, it's time for bed,
As ocean fish dance overhead.
Moonlit waters, a soft embrace,
Lullabies in this magical place.

So close your eyes, let worries flee,
For the sea's sweet laughter, wild and free.
Each wave cradles in gentle sway,
A funny bedtime, come what may.

Sunlit Serenity

Waves giggle as they race,
Splashing sand all over the place.
Seagulls squawk with a silly cheer,
Dancing round, oh so near.

Sunbeams tickle the azure blue,
As flip-flops fly like birds that flew.
Sunbathers make strange sun shapes,
While sunscreen rescues from bad scrapes.

Buckets filled with dreams and sand,
Children building castles, oh so grand.
But watch out for the sneaky tide,
It sneaks in fast, like a mischievous slide!

With laughter echoing on the shore,
Life is a game, who could ask for more?
The sun's merry rays make us sway,
In this cheerful seaside ballet.

Chasing Horizon's Glow

Crabs perform a dance, so absurd,
While fisherman sings to a flying bird.
With nets all tangled, a fishy plight,
A seagull swoops in, what a sight!

Surfboards stand like soldiers in a line,
As surfers try to catch a wave divine.
Yet nose dives cause quite the messy splash,
In this watery world, they flop and thrash.

Shells and starfish hold a board game there,
Laughing at beachgoers with messy hair.
Who knew a beach trip would lead to this?
Laughter lingers like a salty kiss.

As the sun sinks low, colors collide,
With joy and laughter, it's fun to bide.
Chasing after rays, one big happy row,
In this playful paradise, we overflow!

Beneath a Sapphire Sky

Kites dance high in the playful breeze,
As kids chase waves while climbing trees.
Sandy footprints leading nowhere fast,
And ice cream melts—oh, summer's blast!

Pails of laughter spill on sunlit sand,
While flip-flops slip out of hand.
The sun winks down with a cheeky grin,
As waves slip past, where fun begins.

Mermaids in swimsuits sunbathe with glee,
Who knew a tail could look like a tee?
With jellyfish jokes and seaweed fights,
Every moment brims with delightful sights.

Starfish compete for the silliest pose,
While surfers practice their most epic toes.
Beneath this sapphire sky we reside,
In our world of joy, we shall abide.

Laughter of the Tide

The tide rolls in with a chuckle so bright,
As crabby critters plan their night flight.
A dolphin jumps in a splashy display,
Who knew the sea had so much to say?

Buoys bicker like gossiping foes,
In funny hats made from seashells and hose.
The lifeguard naps, dreaming of bread,
While beach balls bounce on sun-kissed head.

In this merry land where giggles reside,
You'll find joy swaying by the beachside.
With warm waves crashing in silly gasps,
And mermaids giggling through their sand clasps.

So, let's embrace the laughter we find,
In the salty breeze, we're all intertwined.
Join the fun where the sea meets the shore,
Because life's a wave, let's laugh some more!

Ebb and Flow of Solace

The waves tickle toes and tease,
While seagulls plot their next mischief,
A crab sidesteps with panache,
Its dance is quite a sight to see!

An octopus shows off its flair,
With eight arms waving in the breeze,
It grimaces, then makes a face,
Like it's just heard the worst of news!

In the shallows, laughter erupts,
As kids dive in, then whirl like tops,
One floats by with a goofy grin,
A treasure hunt for sand and socks!

But watch out for the sneaky wave,
It's sneaky like a clever foe,
It crashes down, your hat now gone,
The tide's the master of this show!

Sun-Kissed Waters

A sunbeam slips, a slippery ray,
It tickles my nose, oh hey! oh ho!
The beach ball flies, with laughter and cheers,
As sunscreen's applied like a thick mud show!

Flip-flops race as they scamper around,
In a dance-off against the old beach chair,
Sun hats wobble, their fashion a hit,
But they fall off just to play in the air!

The seagulls squawk with too much attitude,
As they prance around like beachside kings,
Stealing fries right from your picnic plate,
Those feathered thieves have no shame, it seems!

With laughter echoing in the waves,
We chase the tides with childish glee,
And in this joyful sandy chaos,
Who knew that fun would cost a fee?

Breezes that Sing

A gentle breeze hums sweet refrains,
It rustles through the palm trees' hair,
Whispers secrets to my sandcastle,
While bringing a crab to dance with flair!

The kites fly high, like fish out of water,
They loop and dive, catching the sky,
With tails that swirl like seaweed canceled,
It's a flight school just waiting to try!

Waves giggle as they rush to the shore,
They tickle my ankles then run away,
In a playful game of tag and tease,
I stomp and splash, but they refuse to stay!

But amidst the splashes and the fun,
The sea foam winks with a bubbly tone,
And all the world with joy and laughter,
Is simply a merry ocean zone!

Reflections in the Teal

Water glimmers as it reflects,
A mirror to the chaos near,
My sunglasses hide my eyes so sly,
A secret life of summer cheer!

Mermaids swim with flicks and twists,
While dolphins play hide and seek,
They leap and laugh, poking fun,
At the humans below, so meek!

Sandcastles rise like royal towers,
But the tide is plotting, don't you know,
It giggles softly as it creeps,
Quick! The flag's gone, where did it go?

With all these shenanigans at play,
The beach, a circus of delight,
Who knew a dip could lead to chuckles,
And tides can spark a lively night!

Currents of Calm

A fish with dreams of being cool,
Wearing shades, it's breaking rules.
It dives in style, gives a little flip,
While a crab serves drinks with a gestures hip.

The jellyfish dance in a wobbly way,
With glow sticks, they light up the bay.
The whale sings low with a laugh so loud,
While the sea turtles gather, feeling proud.

An octopus juggling shells and flotsam,
Wonders if he should join a dance jam.
The starfish claps with all ten arms,
Saying, "This is where we find all charms!"

Fish flip-flop in a disco style,
The plankton groove, they're full of guile.
They twirl around, and the bubbles cheer,
In a sea so bright, there's nothing to fear.

Embracing the Aquatic Light

A dolphin wearing a bright pink hat,
Says, "Look at me, I'm a fancy cat!"
With a flip and a splash, he steals the show,
In the shimmering sea, putting on a glow.

A seagull yells, "Watch your lunch, mate!"
As the fish throw a party at half-past eight.
They dance on waves and twirl about,
Who needs a plate when you've got a route?

Anemones giggle in fields of foam,
Playing hide and seek in their underwater home.
They tickle unsuspecting fish as they pass,
With arms spread wide, they share a laugh.

The crabs host a ball with a conch shell band,
While the plankton whirl like a glittery sand.
In this quirky world, it's never a bore,
As they twirl in the light that they all adore.

Warm Encounters with the Deep

A walrus sporting a funky tie,
Tells the seals, "Let's swim and fly!"
With belly bumps and laughter so sweet,
They surf the waves, just feeling the beat.

The pufferfish puffs with a giggly grin,
Says, "I'm not scared, let the fun begin!"
With a flip of his fins, he spins around,
Blowing bubbles that go up and down.

The clownfish jokes in vivid hues,
Creating laughter, it's never old news.
"Come dance in the sea, let's make a splash!"
While a sea cucumber watches in a flash.

A pod of dolphins in a conga line,
Celebrate life under sunshine divine.
With joy and delight, they splash and play,
The deep blue giggles, come join the fray!

The Radiant Shoreline

On the beach where crabs make friends,
One digs a hole, the other pretends.
"Let's build a castle!" one shouts in glee,
While the waves keep crashing, full of jubilee.

With sun hats on, they start to race,
Making a mess at a frantic pace.
A seagull swoops down for a salty snack,
Laughing so hard, it nearly falls back!

A starfish joins with a sunblock dab,
"Don't fry in the sun, that's not a fab grab!"
They roll in the sand, making funny shapes,
As the tide pulls back and the shoreline shakes.

With laughter echoing far and wide,
On this radiant shore, they take in the tide.
Every moment filled with joy and cheer,
In this funny world, there's nothing to fear.

Caresses of the Sea Breeze

A seagull swoops, snatches my fries,
While I laugh, trying to act wise.
Sand sticks to my foot like glue,
I swear it's plotting to stay too.

The pier wobbles, I cling on tight,
A crab decides I'm quite a sight.
Splashing waves and giggles blend,
I'm soaked now, but it's a fun trend!

A dolphin leaps, thinks it's a show,
Waves are clapping—what a row!
With salty hair and dreams galore,
Who needs a spa when you can roar?

Laughter dances, bright and loud,
As I trip over a flowered shroud.
Yet here I am, happy and free,
Thanking the breeze for tickling me!

Tranquil Waters at Twilight

The sun dips low, and crabs retreat,
While I dance with my flippered feet.
Starfish giggle, they're quite the crowd,
Underneath waves, they're feeling proud.

My toes get nibbled, fish say hi,
I think they're plotting to make me fry!
The tide pulls back, just like my drink,
I laugh aloud—not a moment to think.

Sailing boats with sails askew,
Yelling, 'Ahoy! What's new with you?'
A pirate parrot squawks in glee,
I chase it all—so full of spree!

Sandcastles crumble, a tidal fate,
But I don't mind, I celebrate!
With laughter echoing, out we sway,
This dusk is wild—hip-hip-hooray!

Canvas of the Nautical Dream

Waves paint laughter on sandy shores,
Each splash tells tales—open doors!
Seashells giggle, oh what a tune,
Shells in my pockets? Quite a boon!

Mermaids twirl, braid their seaweed hair,
Singing fierce songs about sun and air.
Suddenly, a wave crashes high,
Now everyone's got salt in their eye!

I tried to surf—oh what a sight,
Fell flat on my face, but that's alright.
The tide just chuckled, gave me a push,
Now I'm a dolphin, in a big splashy bush!

Beach balls soar like comets here,
I dodge and weave, fueled by cheer.
With crayons of sunset, I paint my world,
In this salty domain, my joy's unfurled!

Where Whales Whisper

Giggles echo as whales swim by,
They're planning a party under the sky.
Mermaids wink from bubbles below,
Inviting me to join their show!

I tried to dive—oh, what a clumsy trip,
But the fish said, 'Welcome, take a dip!'
Lagging behind, I swam like a brick,
But laughter turns even blunders slick!

Flopping seals join in the fun,
With silly faces, they dash and run.
A jellyfish bounces, then gives me a hug,
In this wacky world, I'm snug as a bug.

With giggly friends in the shimmering blue,
I splash and play—adventures anew.
Every whisper, every cheer,
This silly sea holds my heart dear!

The Calm Before the Embrace

The sun peeked out, a shiny grin,
As waves danced wildly, chaos within.
Seagulls squawked, demanding a snack,
While beach balls soared, no one looked back.

A lobster wore shades, looking quite fly,
While kids built castles, reaching the sky.
The tide pulled back, then gave a sly wink,
As surfers spilled drinks and started to sink.

Sandcastles toppled, a jellyfish cheered,
While sunscreen warriors had nothing to fear.
The sand in our toes felt oddly like glue,
Yet laughter erupted, a warm, salty brew.

At sunset, we laughed, our faces aglow,
Chasing crabs swiftly for a good show.
With flip-flops a-flopping, we ran with delight,
The sea's warm embrace, oh, what a sight!

A Symphony of Blue

A symphony plays on the shoreside stage,
Where dolphins and seaweed dance with rage.
The tide's playful whispers, oh what a tune,
While sea urchins clap under the moon.

Mermaids with ukes strum songs so off-key,
While whales hum bass lines, feeling so free.
The ocean's orchestra, a hilarious show,
As jellyfish jam like they're putting on a glow.

Crabs roll in circles, all dressed up to impress,
While barnacles giggle in their little mess.
A clam tried to beatbox, oh what a sight,
As barnacles busted some moves left and right.

With beachgoers laughing, we joined in the fun,
And danced with the fish, till the day was done.
As the curtain fell on our aquatic spree,
We kvelled and we cheered, brought together with glee.

Whispers of the Depths

In the briny blue, secrets are found,
Where fish gossip softly and seaweed is crowned.
An octopus winks with eight arms wide,
As clams plot mischief and giggle with pride.

"Don't take my shell," said one crafty crab,
While bubbles burst forth like a playful jab.
The anglerfish chuckled, lighting the dark,
As snails took a selfie, it turned out quite stark.

The sea turtle strolled with style on his back,
While sea cucumbers planned a surprise attack.
The sand echoed joy, like a raucous ballet,
As underwater critters laughed their day away.

From krill to the sharks, a clique in full swing,
Sharing their wild tales, oh what fun they bring!
In these whispers of depths, laughter prevails,
As we glimpse underwater, where humor never fails.

The Harbor's Heart

In the harbor's heart, where rowboats collide,
With sailors who chatter, their patience a tide.
Fishing poles stand like they're keeping the score,
While gulls steal fries, strutting 'round the shore.

Docks creak with laughter, as nets trip and fall,
And fish swap tall tales on an old wooden wall.
A hermit crab strutted, clad in a shell,
While a fisherman swore he'd caught a fish bell.

Kids splash in puddles, their laughter the waves,
While the fishermen's jokes are the wildest of knaves.
As boats bob up and down, they sing out a tune,
That even the buoys hum along to in June.

As the day winds down, and sunsets begin,
The smile on our faces is impossible to pin.
In the harbor's embrace, we gather to part,
Where memories sparkle, the sea has our heart!

Lighthouses of the Heart

In a lighthouse so bright, a seagull took flight,
With dreams of the fish, oh what a delight.
But tripped on a crab, oh what a mess,
The guard of the sea now in a big dress!

The waves laughed and danced, they couldn't stop,
As the lighthouse keeper dropped his mop.
With a wink and a grin, he let out a cheer,
'Next time I'll teach that gull to adhere!'

The boaters all giggled at the sight they had seen,
A lighthouse so clumsy, it should've been lean.
But in all of its wobbles, it stood proud and tall,
Guiding the lost, keeping fears small.

So here's to the lighthouses, guardians of fun,
With silliness shared under the sun.
May they shine through the laughs and the jests,
For even in laughter, they give us their best!

A Ballet of the Brine

Underwater, fish danced with flair,
A fish in a tutu, what a funny affair!
With pirouettes and twirls, oh how they pranced,
While jellyfish giggled, completely entranced.

A starfish attempted a leap, quite a sight,
But landed on coral, much to its fright!
With flippers and fins, they glided with glee,
'Who needs a partner? Just watch me!'

The turtles applauded, slow as can be,
With a clapping of flippers, so pleased to see.
A show in the waves, so absurd yet divine,
A ballet beneath waves, a twist of design!

So let laughter bubble, like foam on the shore,
With fish in the spotlight, forever encore.
For under the surface, hilarity thrives,
In this ballet of brine, where joy arrives!

Harmony of the Tides

The tides are all tuneful, a splashy delight,
With waves that are singing, through day and night.
A crab with a kazoo, trying to play,
While splashing the seagulls, oh what a display!

Starfish strummed star-songs, harmonica seas,
With a shell and a laugh, floating free as a breeze.
As dolphins chimed in with their playful clicks,
All wrapped up in rhythm, dancing the tricks.

The ocean's a stage with bubbles for sound,
Each splash is a note, harmonies abound.
Even the fishermen, caught in the tune,
Giggled and wiggled beneath the bright moon.

So sing along, dear friends, don't let out a sigh,
For in this wet concert, we'll flounder and fly.
With joy in the depths, it rises and glides,
Welcome the laughter, sweet harmony rides!

The Caress of the Deep

Down in the depths, where giggles arise,
A crab told a joke, much to our surprise.
'Why don't fish ever play cards?' he exclaimed,
'Because they're scared of the sharks, they're too famous to be named!'

The octopus chuckled, tangled up in ink,
While seaweed swayed and began to rethink.
'Come dance with my arms, I'll show you some moves,'
'But don't bother the turtles, they've got their own grooves!'

Blowfish blow bubbles, oh what a sight,
Each pop is a laugh that bounces with light.
As the stingrays slide by, all smooth and suave,
They wink at a fish with a newfound brave!

So sink into laughter, let the current embrace,
In the depths of the sea, where joy finds its space.
For even the creatures that drift and they swim,
Can find the delight in the ocean's sweet whim!

Sandy Hugs

With grains of sand stuck on my feet,
I waddle around looking for a seat.
The beach chairs laugh, they've seen it all,
As I trip and stumble, like a beach ball.

Seagulls squawk, they steal my fries,
I toss them some chips, oh what a prize!
They dance and dive, such culinary kings,
While I chase them down, flapping my wings.

My towel's a sail, my sunblock's a mess,
I apply it thick, just trying to impress.
But I turn into a lobster, oh what a sight,
Craving that seafood, but I'll take a bite!

The waves seem to giggle, the tide rolls in,
As I splash around, trying to swim.
Each wave's a friend, a slippery tease,
I'm surfing on smiles and ocean breeze.

Waves of Tranquility

The waves whisper secrets, soft as a breeze,
They tickle my toes and laugh with ease.
A jellyfish floats by, giving me the wink,
I wonder if it's here for the drink!

My flip-flops are missing, just my luck,
I'm toe-squishing shells like a quirky duck.
The seaweed dances, what a strange sight,
As I trip on my towel, oh what a fright!

Buckets and shovels, a castle to make,
But it crumbles faster than a birthday cake.
I watch it fall down, waves clap in glee,
Guess my architecture lacks a degree!

The sunset's a canvas, smeared with delight,
As I lose my balance, it's quite a sight.
I roll in the sand, embraced by the tide,
Life's full of giggles, it's a wild ride.

Midnight Reflections

The moon takes a dip, in the water so bright,
While I play the moonwalk, under starry light.
My shadow's a dancer, out on the shore,
But the crabs steal the spotlight, I can't ask for more.

The waves croon a tune, a midnight chime,
While I look for creatures, wasting my time.
Each splash is a giggle, each moonbeam a song,
As I fumble through darkness, oh, where do I belong?

A lobster passes by, gives me a wave,
I wonder if it's looking for a rave.
With shells for confetti, and seaweed so green,
We'll dance through the night, a bizarre marine scene!

Under the stars, I trip with a grin,
The fish all are laughing, oh let the fun begin!
Each ripple's a giggle, each tide brings a cheer,
As I rock with the rhythm, it's perfectly clear.

Surfing the Hues of Bliss

With a board beneath me, I'm feeling like pro,
I paddle, I wobble, oh no, here we go!
The wave throws a party, I'm crashing the scene,
A salty surprise from my aquatic routine.

I'm one with the water, or so I claim,
As I tumble and splatter, it's all just a game.
The dolphins are giggling, my ride's such a mess,
With each goofy wipeout, I'm feeling the stress!

Sunburned and flailing, I laugh with delight,
While seagulls dive-bomb and give me a fright.
The sun paints the ocean, a canvas so bright,
As I surf through those hues, clumsy but right!

In this dance with the waves, I find my bliss,
Each splash is a joy, I can't help but miss.
Just me and the ocean, a comedic duet,
With plenty of mishaps, I'll never forget!

Sun-Drenched Dreams

The sun baked my toes in a golden hue,
Seagulls squawked loud, what a hullabaloo!
I lost my cool drink to a wave's wild dance,
Now I'm sipping sand, not great at a glance.

The beach ball bounced like a skipping stone,
But every time I threw it, it bounced on its own.
A crab stole my sandwich, what a bold thief,
Now I'm left with just chips, oh, sweet relief!

The Harbor's Glow

Fishes in boats singing sea shanty songs,
Trying to catch crabs who mischievously throng.
A dolphin just winked at my funny hat,
He laughed as I tripped over my own pet cat.

The lighthouse spins 'round, it's a dizzy delight,
While the barnacles dance in the dim moonlight.
A pirate came by, but he left with my shoe,
Claimed it was treasure, oh, what will I do?

Sheltered by the Blue

I found a conch shell, said 'Hello, my friend!'
But it just echoed back, quite the trend.
The starfish giggled as they wiggled about,
I swear they were trying to help me get out!

My towel turned into a sail in the breeze,
Chasing me down like it's got a degree.
The jellyfish jived to my favorite tune,
Bouncing around like it's dancing in June!

Serenade of the Seafoam

The foamy waves sing with a bubbly cheer,
While I lost my flip-flop, oh dear, oh dear!
A party of crabs is keeping the beat,
They stomp their pincers, it's quite the feat.

A sea turtle winked, said "Join us for a race,"
But my bellyflop splash just cleared the whole space.
The ocean keeps laughing, washing in glee,
As I try to swim, but I'm more like a bee!

Sunlit Shores and Gentle Tides

On the beach, a crab did dance,
With a sideways, silly prance.
Seagulls caw in joyful cheer,
Stealing fries and giving fear.

Children splash with gleeful shouts,
While sunscreen fights, it swirls about.
Sandcastles rise, then fall apart,
A fortress built—a work of art!

A beach ball bounces, oh so high,
Mom gets hit—oh my, oh my!
Laughter weaves through the salty air,
As flip-flops fly without a care.

The sun dips low, a golden hue,
"Who left their towels?"—that's the cue!
With a splash and giggle, we'll retreat,
Tomorrow's fun will be a treat!

Warm Embrace of the Horizon

The tide rolls in, a playful note,
As fish parade in their tiny boat.
Salty foam tickles my toes,
I wonder how far a jellyfish goes!

Flip-flops are lost in the sandy mire,
A quest begins, I'm catching fire.
The sun beats down, so I take a leap,
Forget the worries, dive in deep!

A dolphin leaps, a comical sight,
Winking at kids with delight!
While seagulls squawk a raucous tune,
"Did someone drop a sandwich soon?"

As the day ends in a splashy hue,
Ice cream cones, oh yes, that's due!
Sandy smiles, we really are,
The funniest bunch beneath a star!

Dance of the Mermaid's Heart

Under waves, a tale unfolds,
Mermaids sing of treasure told.
With fins that sparkle, they do sway,
Caught in seaweed, they twirl away!

"Why wear shells?" one mermaid muses,
While another juggles fishy fuses.
A sea turtle joins with a slow addl,
Teaching dance, oh what a rattle!

"Let's have a party," bubbles one,
With oysters clapping, oh what fun!
The starfish play on their ukes,
While clownfish giggle and dance in flukes!

As tides shall turn, our laughter will soar,
The waves keep rhythm, we all adore.
In a shimmering tale of sparkly mirth,
Who knew the sea held such wild girth!

Soliloquy of Seafoam

On the shore, seafoam runs wild,
A bubbly jokester, a frothy child.
It tickles toes and playfully splashes,
While seashells giggle in funny flashes!

"Why don't fish wear a tuxedo?" it asks,
As waves hold court, ignoring their tasks.
"Because they'd look silly! Oh what a sight!"
A blowfish bubbles, "I'm not quite right!"

Tangled seaweed, a wig on the sand,
A crab struts by, it's all quite grand!
While gulls fly high, sharing their snack,
"Watch out below!"—a fishy attack!

As the sun sets, humor won't cease,
The shoreline giggles in joyful peace.
With laughter echoing all through the night,
The beachy whimsy feels just right!

Whims of the Warm Breeze

The seagulls squawk, they steal my fries,
As I chase them down, I trip and rise.
With sand in my shoes and salt in my hair,
I wonder if they even care!

A beach ball bounces, hits my face,
Laughter erupts, I join the race.
With buckets and shovels, we build a pile,
A sandcastle that won't last a while.

The sun shines bright, my skin's a glow,
I try to surf but fall—oh no!
With splashes and giggles, I wade around,
In this merry chaos, joy is found.

The breeze whispers tales of mermaid's glee,
While sunscreen slips, it's just my spree.
A day of fun that leaves me sore,
Yet I can't wait to come back for more!

The Color of Comfort

The towel's too small, I'm all rolled up,
Like a sausage in a paper cup.
With snacks all sandy and drinks that spill,
But laughter's plenty, I've got my fill.

The waves come crashing, oh what a sight!
I pretend to surf, but it doesn't feel right.
With tricks and flips that flop and fail,
I find it's best to just set sail.

A crab walks by, in a snapping mood,
As I attempt to dance, it feels quite crude.
With flip-flops flying, I shuffle around,
In this circus of fun, I'm ocean-bound!

The sunset paints the sky with cheer,
While seagulls plot their dinner in here.
With belly laughs and waves of glee,
Who knew comfort could be so silly?

Whispers of the Tidal Breeze

The breeze whispers softly, as I munch my snack,
But a seagull swoops down, a clever attack.
With popcorn in hand, I leap and I'm caught,
In a game of hurry, oh what a thought!

The beach chair tips, I'm off the ground,
With sand on my back, I look all around.
A sunburned lobster, I laugh at my fate,
Guess sunscreen isn't something I rate!

The waves invite me for a cool dip,
But I splash so much, it feels like a trip.
With giggles and glances, my friends all agree,
Each tumble and slip brings pure jubilee!

As night falls gently, we laugh and we feast,
With stories of blunders, laughter increased.
For in this retreat, soaked in fun,
The humor's the treasure, and we've just begun!

Embrace of Sunny Waves

In bright golden sun, my towel's a nest,
But a rogue wave crashes, oh, what a jest!
Soaked to my bones, I laugh without care,
A little splash fight? I gladly declare!

The kids run wild, their giggles a song,
As they build up castles, things can't go wrong.
The tide rolls in with a playful tease,
Swooshing away their hard-won keys.

With ice cream cones dripping, the flavors all blend,
Chocolate on my nose, oh, what a trend!
The sticky sweet mess is a badge of pride,
In this crazy carnival, I'll take the ride!

As evening approaches, we gather in sight,
With stories and laughter, a delightful night.
Underneath the stars, we sing and we sway,
In the clutch of the tide, we dance and we play!

Currents of Comfort

Waves crash and splash, oh what a scene,
A crab doing the cha-cha, quite the routine!
Seagulls squawk softly, stealing my fries,
As fish flip and flop, under sunny skies.

Sunburned tourists dance with great cheer,
While dolphins make jokes, or so I hear.
Beachballs flying high, like they own the place,
A sandcastle toppled, oh what a disgrace!

Flip-flops are flopping, don't know where to land,
A kid's ice cream drips, right into the sand.
Laughter erupts as we all start to play,
Just watch out for seagulls, they won't hesitate!

With smiles and giggles, we bask in the fun,
Each wave that rolls in feels like a pun.
The sun starts to set, painting skies in a swirl,
As the ocean keeps chuckling, with each little whirl.

Beneath the Salted Sky

Grab your snorkels, let's dive real deep,
Where fish wear bow ties, and chatter while we creep.
A mermaid named Sally has quite the wit,
She ribbits like a frog—oh, what a hit!

Octopuses juggle, like clowns in a show,
While turtles tell tales of where they must go.
Sea cucumbers frolic, just lounging about,
Giving shells the side-eye without a doubt.

Sand dunes in pajamas, and starfish with ties,
Even crabs throw parties under blue skies.
With laughter echoing, we wade through the fun,
Beneath the salty sky, oh what a run!

As waves wash our worries far out and away,
With silly sea pets, we laugh and we play.
In the splash of the tides, let giggles unite,
For beneath this vast sky, every moment's bright!

Serene Sands at Dusk

As the sun paints the beach in hues of gold,
A pelican snorts, just a bit bold.
Sandcastles lean in, gossiping away,
While kids chase the tide like a game of ballet.

Hot dogs are served, a feast on the shore,
As flip-flops fly, leaving marks galore.
Ladies in sun hats, sipping their drinks,
While beach balls bounce, giving everyone winks.

Cool breezes giggle, tickling our noses,
As sand crabs race home, much faster than roses.
We splash and we splash, with no thoughts of dread,
Those sandy toes dancing—it's pure joy ahead!

So come join the party, the fun never ends,
With laughter and play, and maybe some bends.
As daylight fades softly, like an old song,
We swing to the rhythm where we all belong!

Echoes of the Deep Blue

Splash! Crash! A wave brings some laughs,
As jellyfish wiggle, showing off gaffes.
A whale sings a tune, off-key but grand,
While fish line dance with a soft, sandy band.

Surfers keep stumbling, then rise with a cheer,
Dolphins jump ship, they're already here!
A crab peeks around, wearing a bright hat,
As the sun sets in colors, a real magic spat.

Shovels and buckets, a kid's grand parade,
Collecting seashells, some funny charades.
The tickle of waves is nature's own jest,
As we laugh in the splashes, there's no time for rest.

So let's raise our voices, let echoes rebloom,
With fun and with joy, we'll brighten the room.
In the deep blue, we find what's anew,
For laughter and sunshine are always in view!

Marvels of Meditative Shores

Seagulls squawk, what a tune,
They dance around like a cartoon.
Sandcastles rise as dreams take flight,
While crabs upstage, what a sight!

Flip-flops squeak, it's quite a show,
As splashing kids steal the flow.
Sunburned noses, red as can be,
Oh dear sun, you're a joker, you see!

Beach balls soar, then land with a plop,
Sandy snacks make everyone stop.
A dog digs deep, like a goldmine,
Turns out he's just searching for a brine!

Waves tickle toes and splash on the chest,
Laughter erupts, it's simply the best.
Bikini tops fly in the wind's clever game,
While everyone giggles at who's to blame!

Horizon's Lullaby

Clouds float by with a cheeky grin,
It's a contest of who's fluffier within.
Water's like soup, with a pinch of salt,
While dolphins chirp, it's their fault!

Sandy feet shuffle, looking for shells,
Only to find a beach ball's yells.
Seashells whisper secrets of the tide,
While fish wiggle, oh, how they glide!

Picnic spreads, with chips that crunch,
Watch out for seagulls, they'll take your lunch!
Kites fly high, caught in the breeze,
Who knew their strings could twist like these?

Sunset's glow, a painter's delight,
As stars come out, ready for night.
Voices echo, in playful delight,
The sea just chuckles, it's quite the sight!

Tides of Togetherness

Family picnics, what a blast,
Spill the juice, it's a colorful cast.
Tugging at towels, a tug-of-war,
With laughter ringing from the shore!

Buckets and spades, what a fine mix,
Building castles out of old sticks.
Children giggle, as waves chase feet,
Slipping and sliding, oh what a feat!

Splashing about, in a watery dance,
Sunscreen fights turn into a chance.
Chasing each other, who's got the sand?
Looks like everyone's in high demand!

Naptime nears under a big sun hat,
Dreams of mermaids, imagine that!
As the tide hums its humorous tune,
We giggle together, 'neath the lazy moon.

Celestial Waves

Stars above like twinkling eyes,
The moon chuckles, a big surprise.
Crashing waves, like a playful roar,
They whisper secrets, stories of yore.

Beach bonfires and roasting delight,
S'mores turn messy—oh what a sight!
Ghost stories shared, with a friendly fright,
The sea adds echoes, to the night's delight.

Fireflies dance in the warm night air,
While night owls gossip, without a care.
Splashing kids, still full of glee,
Making waves, oh how free they be!

In this joy, as stars align,
Together we laugh, with a cheeky shine.
A night so fun, we won't forget,
Under celestial watch, no regret!

Echoes of Sandy Footprints

Sandcastles lean like tipsy drunks,
The tide tickles toes, while seagulls honk.
Crabs scurry off like tiny hotshots,
And I trip over shells, oh, what a bonk!

A beach ball bounces, a dance in the air,
While sunscreen's scent wafts, sticky and rare.
I slip in my flip-flops, but what do I care?
With laughter like waves, we float without a care.

The cool waves laugh at my awkward dance,
Each splash a reminder of my lost chance.
Sunburns and giggles, a sun-kissed glance,
In this sandy circus, we're lost in a trance.

Finally, as twilight drapes the shoreline,
We gather our treasures, our saltwater shrine.
Today's a grand jest, the sun did align,
Where laughter is gold, and the fun's all divine.

Bonds of the Tide

Salty breezes mess with my hair,
Dancing like dolphins in carefree flair.
A bucket of laughter, my toy and my muse,
With a shovel in hand, what will I choose?

Waves crash like jokes, each wave making sound,
I chase after seafoam like it's newly found.
The sand sticks to my legs in awkward embrace,
As I tumble and giggle, a clumsy slow race.

A beach ball collides with a nearby sunbather,
"Oh dear!" he exclaims, like a startled alligator.
Still, we all howl like it's part of the play,
Our laughter like tides, washing worries away.

As sunset paints skies with a wink and a smile,
We reminisce about fun and the sandy aisle.
In bonds of the tide, we all find our groove,
With chuckles and splashes, we effortlessly move.

Tidal Embrace

The tide's warm hug brings shy sea snails,
Tickling my toes as it weaves little trails.
Shells in my pocket whisper secrets of old,
While crabs play coy, oh, they're cheeky and bold!

Infloat inflatable flamingos so grand,
Are they swimming or just drifting in sand?
With sunscreen slathered all over my face,
I look like a ghost in this brilliant place.

Sunscreens and shenanigans shape our fun games,
While sandpipers shuffle without any aims.
We laugh at our footprints, each one a new plot,
A story of slip-ups, oh goodness, a lot!

As evening descends with a giggle and sigh,
We toast with our drinks to the stars up high.
In tidal embrace, the humor we find,
Makes waves of our laughter, soft and unconfined.

Brilliant Horizons

Waves ripple forth like a cheeky parade,
Where snorts of amusement in sunbeam cascades.
Umbrellas like mushrooms sprout, bright with cheer,
Each wave brings a chuckle, each splash draws near.

My beach towel's a canvas for sand grains to find,
A masterpiece forming of the muddled kind.
Seagulls squawk gossip, while kids run amok,
It's a serenade of giggles, our own comic clock.

Tide pools are artwork, a nature's delight,
Where crabs do the cha-cha, oh what a sight!
With laughter exploding like fireworks bold,
Each moment a treasure, bright stories unfold.

At sunset we gather, our hearts full of glee,
With cereal for dinner, don't judge, it's just me!
Brilliant horizons as the day takes its flight,
We revel in memories, each laugh, a delight.

Singing with the Salt

Seagulls laugh as they dive and swoop,
Fish are dancing in a watery loop.
Crabs clapping claws, in a rhythm neat,
Shells start to chatter, what a funny feat!

Waves tickle toes as they rush to play,
Seashells gossip about the fish ballet.
The sun's got jokes, shining bright on the scene,
While starfish giggle, they're the comedy queens!

Sandcastles wobble, collapsing in grins,
As kids splash about, losing all their wins.
We build and we break, what a hilarious sight,
Beneath the blue sky, everything feels right!

Laughter echoes with each frothy spray,
Who knew being silly could brighten the day?
With salt on our lips and joy in our hearts,
Together we laugh, that's where the fun starts!

Beneath the Surface of Calm

Flippers flail in a synchronized dance,
Fish are gossiping, giving me a glance.
An octopus winks with eight crafty eyes,
While turtles tell tales, oh what a surprise!

A catfish wearing a shiny gold crown,
Claims he's the king of the underwater town.
Crabby old clams, they grumble and grieve,
While jellyfish jiggle, "We never leave!"

Seaweed sways with a humorous flair,
Mermaids are laughing, flipping their hair.
The sea cucumbers join in the jest,
Unfurling their jokes, they're a silly fest!

So if you dive down to this watery glee,
Where secrets and chuckles are part of the spree,
Just know that the calm holds much more than peace,
It thrives with laughter that never does cease!

A Canvas of Gentle Radiance

Colors collide, like fish at a fair,
Each wave a brushstroke, a masterpiece rare.
Shells have their say in this art of the sea,
They giggle and chuckle, just you wait and see!

The dolphins paint smiles with flips and with tricks,
While sea stars twirl, oh, what clever little kicks!
The coral reef hums a curious tune,
As plankton parade under the bright afternoon.

The waves throw confetti, as if to announce,
"Come join in the fun, it's a whimsical bounce!"
With laughter erupting from all that reside,
This canvas of life is a magical ride!

From the sprightly fish to the soft sands' embrace,
This funny seascape holds warmth and grace.
So hang out awhile where the colors collide,
And let every giggle be your joyride!

Flicker of Nautical Bliss

Fireflies spark in the harbor at dusk,
Belly-flopping dolphins, it's all about fun husk.
Sailboats chime in with their playful sails,
As crabs tell tall tales of underwater gales!

The sea says, "Relax, let's dance in a swirl,"
With waves as our partners, we twist and twirl.
Seashells whisper secrets, sharing their glee,
As the fish throw a party—a splendid jubilee!

Barnacles chuckle, they jest and they tease,
With ticklish sea anemones swaying in the breeze.
The horizon stretches, a canvas less meek,
Where laughter and mischief play hide and seek!

So let's ride the waves with a chuckling cheer,
Enjoying the sparkles that shimmer so near.
With every splash, there's a story to kiss,
In this flicker of joy, let's all feel the bliss!

The Sea's Hidden Solace

Beneath the waves, a crab does dance,
In his tiny shell, he takes a chance.
A beach ball floats, it's not a whale,
While seagulls squawk, we tell a tale.

The sunburned folks made quite a scene,
With mismatched socks and shirts of green.
They dig for clams, but what they find,
Is just some sand, and a piece of twine.

A dolphin jumps, a splash, a wink,
"I'm here for fish!" he seems to think.
We laugh so hard, we snort and squeal,
As jellyfish dance—what a surreal deal!

In this salty realm, all worries cease,
With every splash, we find our peace.
So take a dip, come laugh a lot,
In this silly place, we forget our plot.

Driftwood Dreams

A piece of driftwood said with glee,
"I once was a tree, now I'm fancy free!"
With barnacles on, and splashes round,
He holds court here, the wisest found.

Meanwhile, hermit crabs throw a bash,
Wearing new homes made of old glass trash.
They dance in circles, quite the sight,
While minnows giggle, "What a night!"

A rubber duck, loud and proud,
Floats like royalty in the crowd.
"Quack!" he shouts, "Join in my team!
We'll paddle through life, or so it seems!"

The tide rolls in, with fish that prance,
While seaweed sways in a merry dance.
Each splash and laugh, we float on high,
With driftwood dreams, we touch the sky.

Salty Kisses

A wave swirls up, "Come kiss my face!"
While kids scream loud—what a wild race!
They run and leap, then slip, and fall,
With salty grins, they heed the call.

Whales sing songs, and seals reply,
While surfers ride on clouds, oh my!
A crab in shades gives us a cheer,
"Join my beach party—bring some beer!"

Seagulls swoop like they own the place,
Stealing fries with an air of grace.
Our sandwiches vanish, with yet another,
The gulls' high jinks make us laugh, oh brother!

With sun-kissed skin, we lounge around,
Telling salty tales, a joyous sound.
In this seaside spot, our hearts ignite,
With every giggle, life feels just right.

Beyond the Distant Horizon

The horizon calls us to a spree,
With pirate hats, we sail with glee.
Our ship is made of random junk,
But in our hearts, we feel like funk!

A cannon made of soda cans,
We launch our snacks with silly plans.
The fish below are quite bemused,
As chips rain down, they muse and cruise.

A treasure map leads to a surprise—
Empty bottles and seagulls that rise.
"Oh look," we shout, "A goldfish bowl!"
It's just an old can, but that's our role!

So let the waves keep rolling in,
With laughter echoing where we begin.
Beyond that line, we chase our dreams,
In this fun-filled world, it's not as it seems!

Melodies on the Shoreline

Seagulls sing in the air,
Crabs do a funky dance,
Waves clap hands with delight,
While starfish take a chance.

Sandcastles rise up high,
Only to meet their fate,
As toddlers run with glee,
Chasing seashells on a plate.

The sun plays hide and seek,
With clouds that look like sheep,
The tide whispers silly jokes,
As kids drift off to sleep.

In the water, sharks wear ties,
And dolphins swim with style,
A fish in a top hat grins,
Making all the beachgoers smile.

Dance of Secrets in Blue

In deep waters, fish hold hands,
They twirl 'round coral trees,
Seaweed sways like hipster bands,
As crabs chill with cool breeze.

Octopuses do the twist,
While eels show off their flair,
Turtles join the ocean's fist,
And float without a care.

The jellies float like balloons,
With jellybeans in tow,
As dolphins play the maroons,
Making waves steal the show.

A secret dance beneath the blue,
Where laughter blends with splash,
And every wave is a debut,
In this underwater bash!

A Warmth like the Sun

Sandy shorts and ice cream cones,
Laughter echoes in the breeze,
The beach balls fly like drones,
While seagulls try to tease.

Sunbathers lie like happy logs,
With flip-flops lost from view,
Hot dogs laugh in ketchup bogs,
While salty fries dance too.

Sandwiches dressed like sumo men,
Wrestling crumbs to the ground,
As sunscreen fights to hold the tan,
With laughter all around.

At dusk the beach becomes a stage,
As shadows play their game,
And every wave is a new page,
In the sun's golden name.

Tide Pools of Tranquility

Tiny worlds in clear glass bowls,
Where crabs wear tiny shoes,
Starfish tell the funniest trolls,
While seashells sip on brews.

A clam's got jokes that crack the shell,
As oysters play a tune,
The sea anemones do well,
Throwing parties in the afternoon.

Each tide pool hides some funny finds,
Like sea cucumbers that jest,
And wink with slippery behinds,
At the bird who stole their nest.

In these pools, the laughter swells,
With each glimmering tide,
Nature's jokes and secret spells,
Reveal the joy inside.

The Harbor's Kindness

A seagull stole my sandwich, oh dear,
With a squawk and a flap, disappear!
The boat bobbed like a playful pup,
As I chased my lunch, never gave up.

A fisherman's pole got caught in my hat,
He laughed so hard, said, 'A fish isn't that fat!'
Waves lapped gently at my wet feet,
In this harbor of laughter, life's a treat!

I saw a crab do a silly little dance,
Twisting and turning, oh, what a chance!
With a splash and a giggle, it scuttled away,
I vowed to join it for the next coastal ballet!

Amidst all the chaos, we share a grin,
Who knew such joy could come from a fin?
With the sun shining bright and spirits high,
This harbor's kindness makes worries goodbye!

Oceanside Serenity

At the shore, I found a lost flip-flop,
Waved at a wave, and it gave a plop!
Sandcastles crumbled, what a sight,
As kids yelled, 'It's just a sandy plight!'

In a beach chair, a sunburnt dad snoozed,
While his ice cream cone was thoroughly bruised.
Seagulls plotted, flying high above,
To snag that treat, oh, how they covet love!

Shells were collected with grand hopes and dreams,
But a hermit crab stole them, or so it seems.
With laughter and joy all around the bend,
This shore could use a little mirth to lend.

So here we sit, toes in the sand,
Joking and laughing, and it's all quite grand.
The waves keep rolling, a comical spree,
In oceanside serenity, pure jubilee!

Ripples of Joy

I tossed a pebble and watched it spin,
It made a splash that caused a din!
The ducks all quacked, their feathers quite ruffled,
As the water danced; the laughter shuffled.

A child with a bucket cried, 'It's a whale!'
But it turned out to be a stray piece of mail.
The beach ball soared high, then dropped with a flop,
Landed near my head, then rolled to a stop!

Jellyfish floated, sporting a grin,
As surfers rode waves; chaos to win!
Splashing and giggling, no frowns in sight,
These ripples of joy bring pure delight!

The tide in its wisdom holds stories untold,
Of laughter and fun, of memories bold.
From shore to shoreline, the joy will flow,
With every soft whisper and playful blow!

Glow of the Setting Sun

The setting sun wore a crown of gold,
While beachgoers clapped, their laughter uncontrolled.
A dog chased its tail, what fun to behold,
As seagulls squabbled due to crumbs uncontrolled!

A yoga class tried to find a calm pose,
But a kid yelled, 'Boo!' and it fell like a rose.
With giggles and chuckles, they joined in the fun,
Twisting and turning, oh, what a run!

As the sun dipped low, colors swirled bright,
While kids built bonfires, igniting the night.
Marshmallows roasted, sticky and sweet,
With stories and fun, oh, a treat to repeat!

So here we gather, the day's final cheer,
With warmth all around and laughter sincere.
As the sun loses fight, but brightens the dune,
We'll dance and we'll sing to the glow of the moon!